DO THE WORK!
GOOD HEALTH AND WELL-BEING

COMMITTING TO THE UN'S SUSTAINABLE DEVELOPMENT GOALS

JULIE KNUTSON

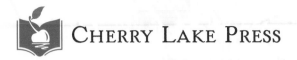
CHERRY LAKE PRESS

Published in the United States of America by Cherry Lake Publishing Group
Ann Arbor, Michigan
www.cherrylakepublishing.com

Reading Adviser: Beth Walker Gambro, MS, Ed., Reading Consultant, Yorkville, IL
Photo Credits: © Take A Pix Media/Shutterstock.com, cover, 1; © Rawpixel.com/Shutterstock.com, 5, 20, 24, 27; Infographic From The Sustainable Development Goals Report 2020, by United Nations Department of Economic and Social Affairs © 2020 United Nations. Reprinted with the permission of the United Nations, 7; © BalkansCat/ Shutterstock.com, 10; © Roman Chazov/Shutterstock.com, 13; © Juice Verve/Shutterstock.com, 14; © Sorn340 Studio Images/Shutterstock.com, 15; © DC Studio/Shutterstock.com, 16; © wavebreakmedia/ Shutterstock.com, 19; © SUPERMAO/Shutterstock.com, 21; © Monkey Business Images/Shutterstock.com, 23; © May Preechaya/Shutterstock.com, 28

Cherry Lake Press is an imprint of Cherry Lake Publishing Group.

Library of Congress Cataloging-in-Publication Data
Names: Knutson, Julie, author.
Title: Do the work! : good health and well-being / by Julie Knutson.
Description: Ann Arbor, Michigan : Cherry Lake Publishing, 2022. | Series: Committing to the
    UN's sustainable development goals | Audience: Grades 4-6
Identifiers: LCCN 2021036390 (print) | LCCN 2021036391 (ebook) | ISBN 9781534199255 (hardcover) |
    ISBN 9781668900390 (paperback) | ISBN 9781668901830 (pdf) | ISBN 9781668906156 (ebook)
Subjects: LCSH: Quality of life—Juvenile literature. | Well-being—Juvenile literature. | Health—Juvenile literature.
Classification: LCC HN25 .K648 2022 (print) | LCC HN25 (ebook) | DDC 301—dc23
LC record available at https://lccn.loc.gov/2021036390
LC ebook record available at https://lccn.loc.gov/2021036391

Cherry Lake Publishing Group would like to acknowledge the work of the Partnership for 21st Century Learning, a Network of Battelle for Kids. Please visit http://www.battelleforkids.org/networks/p21 for more information.

Printed in the United States of America
Corporate Graphics

ABOUT THE AUTHOR

Julie Knutson is an author-educator who writes extensively about global citizenship and the Sustainable Development Goals. Her previous book, *Global Citizenship: Engage in the Politics of a Changing World* (Nomad Press, 2020), introduces key concepts about 21st-century interconnectedness to middle grade and high school readers. She hopes that this series will inspire young readers to take action and embrace their roles as changemakers in the world.

TABLE OF CONTENTS

CHAPTER 1

Meet the SDGs

Just how important are good health and well-being? When people are ill—and when **contagious** diseases like COVID-19 reach **pandemic** scale—we all suffer. Family members might get sick. Schools might close. People may find themselves without work and unable to pay bills. Good health and well-being affect every aspect of society, in every corner of the globe, to different degrees and in different ways.

Across the world, millions of people work to improve health in their communities. Some are nurses and doctors. Others are teachers, city planners, eldercare aides, and volunteers. They are all united by a common goal. They hope to achieve a world in which all people can enjoy healthy lives and a sense of well-being.

Good health and well-being impact everyone.

You can join them! Read on to learn how you can help make the **United Nations**' (UN) third **Sustainable** Development Goal (SDG), "Good Health and Well-Being," a reality.

STOP AND THINK: *Think about the people in your life. Do you know anyone who contributes to health through their work? They don't have to be hospital workers! They could be gym teachers, nursing home workers, school counselors, or community gardeners. Make a list of individuals you know who work or volunteer in this area!*

What Are the SDGs?

In 2015, the United Nations released the 17 SDGs. The SDGs range from "No Poverty" (SDG 1) to "Climate Action" (SDG 13). At the core, these 17 goals are about making life better now and in the future for "people and the planet." All 191 UN member states have agreed to cooperate in reaching the 169 SDG targets by 2030.

"Good Health and Well-Being" is the third goal on the list. It wants to "ensure healthy lives and promote well-being for all at all ages." This means making sure that everyone has the tools, knowledge, and resources needed to live well. It means reducing **chronic** health problems like asthma, fighting preventable diseases, and raising mental health awareness.

Defining Good Health and Well-Being

Just what does it mean to have good health? As the World Health Organization (WHO) puts it, "Health is a state of complete physical, mental, and social well-being and not merely the absence of disease or **infirmity**." In other words, good health is about more than just not being sick. The WHO also notes that the right to health is a fundamental human right. All people—regardless of their race, **ethnicity**, religion, country, or income—should be able to access needed care and resources like **vaccines**.

3 GOOD HEALTH AND WELL-BEING

ENSURE HEALTHY LIVES AND PROMOTE WELL-BEING FOR ALL AT ALL AGES

BEFORE COVID-19

PROGRESS IN MANY HEALTH AREAS CONTINUED, BUT
NEEDS ACCELERATION

CHILD HEALTH   MATERNAL HEALTH   HIV

TUBERCULOSIS   IMMUNIZATIONS

COVID-19 IMPLICATIONS

HEALTHCARE DISRUPTIONS COULD
REVERSE DECADES OF IMPROVEMENTS

HUNDREDS OF THOUSANDS OF ADDITIONAL UNDER-5 DEATHS MAY BE EXPECTED IN 2020

THE PANDEMIC HAS
INTERRUPTED CHILDHOOD IMMUNIZATION PROGRAMMES
IN AROUND
70 COUNTRIES

ILLNESS AND DEATHS
FROM COMMUNICABLE DISEASES
— WILL SPIKE —

SERVICE CANCELLATIONS WILL LEAD TO
100% INCREASE
IN MALARIA DEATHS
IN SUB-SAHARAN AFRICA

LESS THAN HALF
OF THE GLOBAL POPULATION

IS COVERED BY
ESSENTIAL HEALTH SERVICES
(2017)

SUSTAINABLE DEVELOPMENT GOALS

This leads us to a key concept of SDG 3—**equity**. As public health experts at the George Washington University explain, equity requires that we recognize "that each person has different circumstances." Solutions to the lack of good health and well-being are designed with that knowledge in mind. Different resources and opportunities are provided to people based on their location and circumstances. The end goal is a more equal outcome for all.

Here's an example of how this works. Saying that a vaccine is free and available for all on a Tuesday from 9:00 a.m. until 1:00 p.m. is an example of *equality*. All people are offered the same resource. But what if it's only available at one hospital in one part of town? What if you need time off work? What if you need a car to get there? What if this is the *only time* it's offered? What if the site isn't accessible for people with physical disabilities? Making that vaccine available at community clinics in easy-to-reach locations, at a variety of times to meet the needs of working people, is a step toward *equity*.

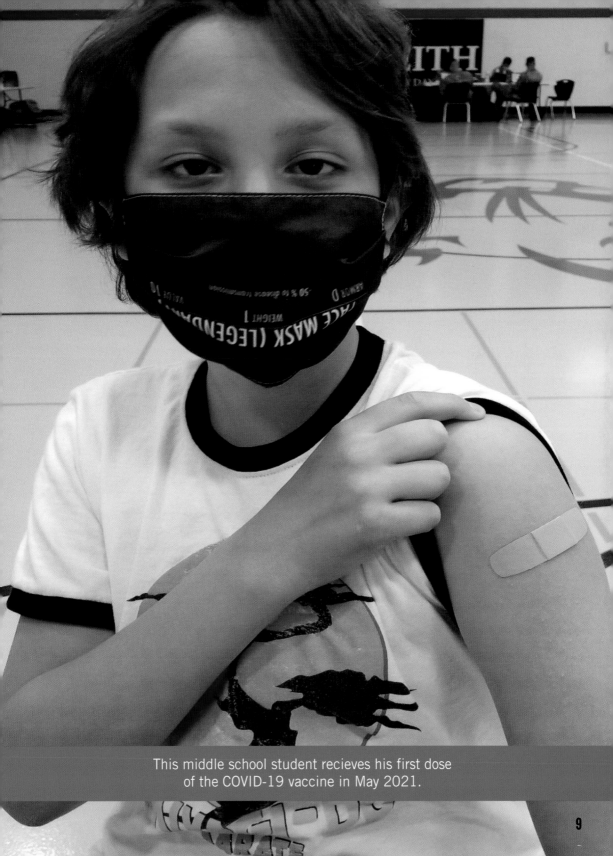

This middle school student recieves his first dose
of the COVID-19 vaccine in May 2021.

Doctors Without Borders has touched millions of lives around the world.

Related Goals

As you look at the full list of SDGs, you'll notice a lot of overlap between goals. "Good Health and Well-Being" doesn't exist in isolation. Work in other goal areas—particularly "No Poverty," "Zero Hunger," and "Clean Water and Sanitation"—can greatly improve the health of millions of the world's people. Action on climate can lessen the amount of air pollution, reducing the number of people with asthma and certain cancers. Creating sustainable cities and communities can provide more opportunities for people to walk, bike, and socialize outdoors. This benefits not just physical health, but also mental and social well-being!

Action on SDG 3 will have direct benefits for people worldwide. It will also create a world in which everyone can have a healthy lifestyle and access to quality health care. Let's get started. Read on to learn more about how you can help build healthier communities!

Doctors Without Borders

Equity is central to the mission of the organization Doctors Without Borders. Founded in France as Médecins Sans Frontières (MSF) in 1971, MSF provides medical aid and **humanitarian** relief where it is most urgently needed. MSF-trained staff work in conflict and war zones. They also help people after disasters like hurricanes and earthquakes.

Today, it operates in 28 countries and employs more than 30,000 people. It's estimated that MSF **personnel** have treated more than 100 million patients since it was established. The organization received the Nobel Peace Prize in 1999.

CHAPTER 2

Why Do We Have Goals?

Have you ever set a New Year's resolution? Or started off the school year with a promise to try a new sport, learn an instrument, or get an "A" in math? If so, you're an experienced goal-setter!

Just as people set goals, so do big organizations like the UN. Whether you are one person or thousands of people working together, there are some solid guidelines for setting and achieving goals. Breaking down the goal into smaller parts is typically the first step in moving from idea to action. The acronym "SMART," which stands for Specific, Measurable, Achievable, Relevant, and Timed, can help both people and organizations meet their goals.

STOP AND THINK: *What goals do you have? How could you use the SMART strategy to reach them?*

It's important to have goals for your health and fitness.

Maternal mortality declined by 38 percent between 2000 and 2017.

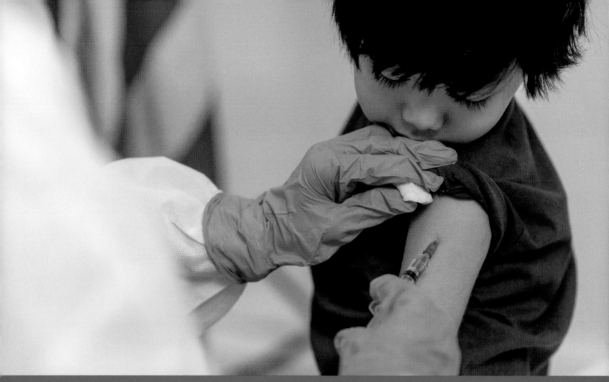

Vaccines can help end childhood deaths. But COVID-19 has interrupted vaccine programs worldwide.

SDG 3 breaks down into 13 smaller targets—"goals within goals"—each of which relates to health and wellness. Examples of those targets include making sure that pregnant women can deliver their babies in safe and healthy environments. Other targets concern educating people about addiction and ending preventable deaths in children under age 5.

You don't have to be a doctor, nurse, counselor, or teacher to make a difference on SDG 3. There are things that you can do—starting today—to make "Good Health and Well-Being" a reality at home, at school, and in your community. Read on to find out how you can be a changemaker.

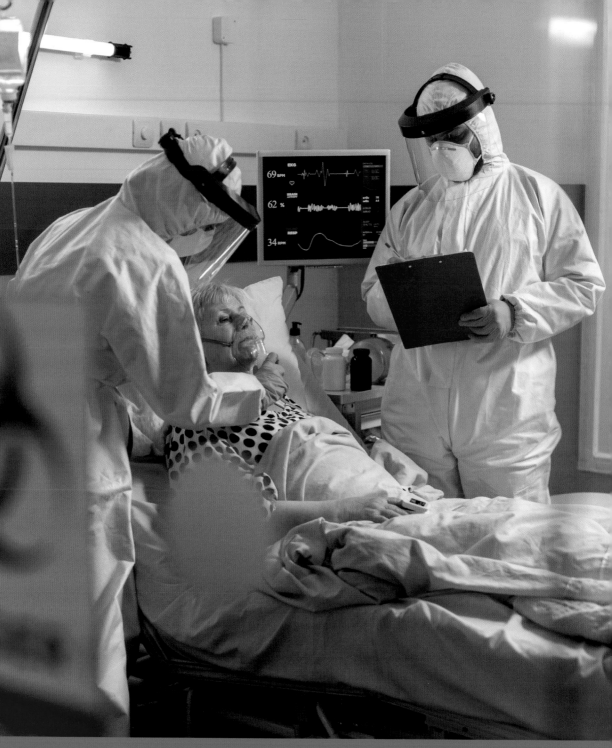

A 2021 review by the WHO found that the COVID-19 pandemic was preventable. A lack of response and preparedness is partially to blame.

Goal 3 Targets

What targets are included under SDG 3? Here's a handy list that explains some of the targets:

- **Safe and healthy childbirth:** This means providing safe, clean, and healthy birthing areas for mothers and babies.
- **End preventable deaths under 5:** Vaccines and access to healthy, nutritious food can help end early childhood deaths. Much progress had been made in this area. The number of under-5 deaths dropped from 9.8 million in 2000 to 5.4 million in 2017.
- **Protect people from preventable diseases:** Governments and people can take measures to halt epidemics and preventable diseases in their tracks!
- **Reduce deaths from noncommunicable diseases:** Globally, 71 percent of deaths each year are due to chronic, **noncommunicable** diseases like diabetes and heart disease. Changes in lifestyle can help reduce this number.
- **Promote mental health:** Anxiety, depression, and attention difficulties are common. Many tactics can help people facing these challenges, especially talking honestly, openly, and nonjudgmentally about them!

CHAPTER 3

Do the Work! Contribute to the Goals at Home

The first step in achieving "Good Health and Well-Being" begins at home, and it starts with you. You and your family can do many things to take care of yourselves. Exercising, managing stress, and getting enough sleep are at the top of the list. Encourage your loved ones to do the same!

Beyond that, there are other ways that you can contribute to SDG 3:

- **Educate** — Knowledge is power! Take what you know and share it with your family members, friends, and neighbors. Get plenty of exercise, and ask others to join you. Walk or bike when you can. If you have family members who smoke, encourage them to stop. And encourage those around you to get vaccinations for preventable illnesses.

A healthy diet is important to feeling your best.

Exercising or playing your favorite sport can help relieve stress.

No matter your age, stretching can help you feel good and prevent injury!

- **Be Kind** — As mentioned earlier, good health is about more than just "not being sick." Feeling a sense of safety and security is key to wellness. Promote well-being by being kind to the people in your life.
- **Deal with Stress** — Research coping strategies that can help when you feel stressed. It might be as simple as taking deep breaths. It could be squeezing a stress ball. Or it might be drawing, jumping on a trampoline, or focusing on the sights and sounds around you. Find what works for you, and use it!

CHAPTER 4

Do the Work! Contribute to the Goals at School

In March 2021, fourth graders at a California elementary school raised $50,000 to support specialty pediatric care at Northern California Shriners Hospital. They gathered donations from people in every single state, including from pro skateboarder Tony Hawk! How did they do it? By working with their teacher to issue challenges and fundraise through social media on TikTok.

Just like these students, you can educate, volunteer, and fundraise to make progress on SDG 3:

- **Educate** — Talk with your teachers to see if you can invite guests to talk about good health and well-being! Visitors could be in-person or virtual and could work in a range of fields. They might talk about what it's like to be a nurse or doctor or about why green spaces are important to healthy communities. The options are many!

You and your classmates could visit a nursing home.

- **Volunteer** — Help create a school environment that promotes well-being for all students. Investigate **peer mediation** programs that help resolve conflict between students. Create anti-bullying posters and messages to remind your peers to treat each other with kindness. Consider hosting an event like a "Mix It Up" lunch day! Sponsored by the organization Learning for Justice, Mix It Up encourages students to sit with other students and make new friends.

What other school fundraising ideas do you have?

- **Fundraise** — Your class can fundraise for local children's hospitals, international organizations like Doctors Without Borders, or groups like the YMCA, which promote overall community health. The Children's Hospital of Richmond recommends these ideas:

— *Penny Drive:* Each classroom collects spare change for donations.

— *Walk/Run During Gym Class:* Hold a school-wide walk/run to raise funds. You can ask family, neighbors, and community members such as your doctor or dentist to sponsor you. Plus, by walking and running, you're maintaining and improving your own health!

— *Car Wash:* With adults such as parents or teachers, hold a community car wash and ask for donations to an organization that promotes good health.

— *Movie Night:* Invite students and their families to watch a movie at the school. You can collect donations as they arrive. Consider hosting a concession stand during the movie to raise more funds.

CHAPTER 5

Do the Work!
Contribute to the Goals
in Your Community

Many of the things that you can do at home and at school to promote SDG 3 can also be done in your community. What else can you do?

- **Advocate** — Write to your elected officials. Tell them to support policies and programs that support the good health and well-being of all community members. Urge them to continue to build **infrastructure** like bike paths and green spaces in all parts of your town, support health care for all, and promote mental health services.

> **STOP AND THINK:** *What details could you include in a letter to an elected official to make a convincing argument on behalf of a cause? What makes for good evidence in support of a program or service?*

Community green spaces provide a place for people to gather in nature.

- **Volunteer** — You and your friends can help build healthier communities. Research volunteer opportunities in an area of interest to you. Maybe it's doing trail repair with your local park district so that more people can exercise outdoors. There are plenty of options!

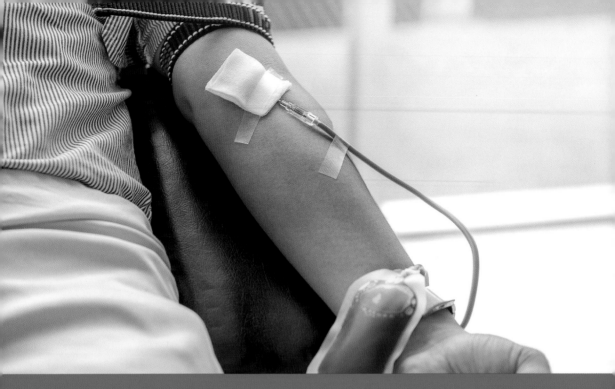

Around 6.8 million people donate blood each year in the United States.

- **Encourage** — Encourage the adults in your life to donate blood. As the WHO states, "Blood is the most precious gift that anyone can give to another person—the gift of life. A decision to donate your blood can save a life, or even several if your blood is separated into its components."

Extend Your Learning

Background

Theater and performance are great ways to share what you know with family, friends, classmates, and neighbors. Write a short play about SDG 3 to share its importance with people in your community.

Act

Think about what you've learned about SDG 3. What do you want other people to know? How can you present this information in a creative, fun way? Here are some questions and ideas to get you started:

- Who will be the characters in your performance?
- What will the setting be?
- What SDG 3 issues will the performance address?
- How will the performance educate the audience about actions they can take regarding SDG 3?

Further Research

BOOKS

Brundle, Joanna. *Vaccines.* Berkeley Heights, NJ: Enslow Publishing, 2021.

Marsico, Katie. *Doctors without Borders.* Ann Arbor, MI: Cherry Lake Publishing, 2015.

WEBSITES

Goal 3: Ensure Healthy Lives and Promote Well-Being for All at All Ages—United Nations Sustainable Development
https://www.un.org/sustainabledevelopment/health
Check out the UN's Sustainable Development Goals website for more information on Goal 3.

The Global Goals of Sustainable Development
margreetdeheer.com/eng/globalgoals.html
Check out these free comics about the UN's Sustainable Development Goals.

Glossary

chronic (KRAH-nik) long-lasting and difficult to get rid of

contagious (kuhn-TAY-juhss) easily spread

equity (EH-kwuh-tee) fairness in distributing opportunities and resources

ethnicity (eth-NIH-suh-tee) belonging to a social group with common national or cultural traditions

humanitarian (hyoo-mah-nuh-TAIR-ee-uhn) benefiting human welfare

infirmity (in-FUHR-muh-tee) illness

infrastructure (IN-fruh-struhk-chuhr) basic physical and operational needs for society to operate, such as roads and bridges

maternal mortality (muh-TUHR-nuhl mor-TAH-luh-tee) when a woman dies during pregnancy or childbirth

noncommunicable (non-kuh-MYOO-nih-kuh-buhl) not contagious from one person to another

pandemic (pan-DEH-mik) a disease prevalent across the whole world

peer mediation (PIHR mee-dee-AY-shuhn) a system for resolving conflicts between peers

personnel (puhr-suh-NEL) a person who works for an organization

sustainable (suh-STAY-nuh-buhl) able to be maintained at a certain rate

United Nations (yuh-NYE-tuhd NAY-shuhns) the international organization that promotes peace and cooperation among nations

vaccines (vak-SEENZ) products that help build a person's immune system and protect against disease

INDEX